Art is 4 Everyone: Art Education Lessons

Including S.T.E.A.M. Lessons

Volume #2: Third Grade - Fifth Grade

Caroline F. Wilson, Ed. D.

Copyright © 2018 Caroline F. Wilson, Ed. D.

All rights reserved.

ISBN: 1986069761
ISBN-13: 978-1986069762

-This book is dedicated to our daughter, E.W. and my art students who have dazzled and inspired with their creativity and "outside of the box" thinking. You are the future!

CONTENTS

	Acknowledgments	vi
	Introduction	1
1	Science + Art	3
2	Technology + Art	39
3	Engineering + Art	51
4	Mathematics + Art	69
5	Substitute/Rainy Day	83
	Appendix A	99
	Appendix B	102
	Appendix C	103
	Appendix D	104
	About the Author	105

ACKNOWLEDGMENTS

This book has been years in the making. My students have provided inspiration through their talents and hard work. It is my fondest wish that future educators and students may benefit from the lessons contained in this text.

Special thanks to my family—especially my husband and daughter, for their support through the process of creating *Art is 4 Everyone: Art Education Lessons*. Together, they support and encourage me—making all things possible.

INTRODUCTION

Students do well when they have a strong academic foundation. Art education contributes to the robust development of every child not only by instilling creativity and providing a healthy expressive outlet, but by reinforcing core educational subjects and concepts. This book seeks to provide educators and parents a resource to further develop their student's abilities through enjoyable S.T.E.M. + Art Education activities.

Collaboration between art education and the fields of Science, Technology, Engineering, and Mathematics is a natural relationship. Creativity is a bound in S.T.E.M. fields of study. Linking art with these core subjects is mutually beneficial. The S.T.E.M. disciplines are faced with many issues and challenges which may be solved with creativity and "outside the box" thinking. By providing students with a strong foundation of intermingling the fine arts with core subject areas, learners will be prepared to creatively innovate when the time is appropriate.

Located in this text are Third, Fourth, and Fifth grade S.T.E.M. + Art Education lessons. The lesson objectives are meant to be a guideline and do not exclusively apply to one state's standards. Lessons in this book use the Virginia Department of Public Education state curriculum. Many aspects of these objectives are interchangeable with your individual state's lesson objectives.

In addition to the S.T.E.M. + Art Education lessons are: substitute/rainy day lesson plans, ideas for assessments for each individual lesson, and sample rubrics located in the text appendices. For more lessons and information, please see Volume #1 and Volume #3 of this text. Inclusion of recommended student reading material and video section does not imply an endorsement of this text by such authors/producers. Thank you and let us remember, "Art is 4 EVERYONE!"

1 SCIENCE + ART

Science: Animal Drawings

Objectives: 3rd Grade

- The student will describe and use steps of the art making process, including brainstorming, preliminary sketching, and planning, to create works of art. (Visual Art 3.2)
- The student will use imaginative and expressive strategies to create works of art. (Visual Art 3.4)
- The student will create works of art that communicate ideas, themes, and feelings. (Visual Art 3.6)
- The student will use organic and geometric shapes in observational drawing. (Visual Art 3.8)
- The student will identify common characteristics of various art careers. (Visual Art 3.17)
- The student will analyze personal works of art, using elements of art and principles of design. (Visual Art 3.19)
- The student will express informed judgments about works of art. (Visual Art 3.20)
- The student will develop and describe personal reasons for valuing works of art. (Visual Art 3.23)
- The student will investigate and understand that adaptations allow animals to satisfy life needs and respond to the environment. Key concepts include: behavioral adaptations; and physical adaptations. (Science 3.4)
- The student will investigate and understand basic patterns and cycles occurring in nature. Key concepts include: animal life cycles. (Science 3.8)

Vocabulary: Echo Lines, Composition, Line, and Repetition

Materials: -8.5" x 8.5" White construction paper -Gel and regular markers -Ruler -Pencil -Black "Sharpie" -Eraser -Newsprint

Procedure:

1) Discuss animals and their habitats after books are read (see below).
2) Students draw 3 animals (hand size) on newsprint. Students may use the "How to Draw" books for ideas (not for tracing)!
3) While students are drawing, class discusses professions related to drawing: art teacher, illustrator, graphic designer, animator, industrial designer, architect, etc.
4) Students choose one of their drawings and get teacher approval for the next step.
5) Trace over it with black "Sharpie."
6) Using pencil, trace (transfer) the animal to the white square.
7) Trace over this animal with "Sharpie."
8) Erase pencil marks.
9) Color animal in with markers.
10) Around the animal (for the background) students may: use the ruler and create a square within a square for a "frame" around their animal, they can add echo lines, add shapes/designs around animal, or place the animal in their habitat.

11) Color in white space and/or add pattern.
12) Mat artwork.
13) Students discuss among tablemates their choices of color and design. They will compare and contrast how each student's work is aesthetically different and that is a celebrated feature of art.

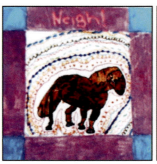  

<u>Recommended student reading</u>:

Frida Kahlo and Her Animalitos by Monica Brown

<u>Recommended student video</u>:

Dropping in on Rousseau by Pamela Geiger Stephens

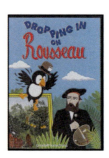

<u>Assessment:</u>

Teacher uses a range of formal and informal assessment strategies to gain insight into students' understanding of lesson, goal achievement, and progress.

Informal:

- Students participate in a class discussion during which questions outlined at the beginning of the lesson are reviewed.
- Individual student-teacher conferences take place during which teacher circulates around classroom assisting students with art project and offering guidance to any questions.
- Teacher observes student work to determine if they used art materials correctly and if they creatively apply skills learned.
- Students participate in a class critique.

Formal:

- Students complete a self-assessment worksheet written in kid-friendly language.
- Teacher completes rubric and uses the tool to evaluate student progress.

**Sample Assessment sheets are located in the book *Appendix*.

Science: Clay Fish/Sharks

Objectives: 3rd Grade

- The student will identify innovative solutions used by artists to solve art-making problems. (Visual Art 3.1)
- The student will use imaginative and expressive strategies to create works of art. (Visual Art 3.4)
- The student will use organic and geometric shapes in observational drawing. (Visual Art 3.8)
- The student will use subtractive and additive processes in various media, including clay, to create sculptures. (Visual Art 3.10)
- The student will analyze personal works of art, using elements of art and principles of design. (Visual Art 3.19)
- The student will express informed judgments about works of art. (Visual Art 3.20)
- The student will develop and describe personal reasons for valuing works of art. (Visual Art 3.23)
- The student will investigate and understand that ecosystems support a diversity of plants and animals that share limited resources. Key concepts include: aquatic ecosystems. (Science 3.6)
- The student will investigate and understand the major components of soil, its origin, and its importance to plants and animals including humans. Key concepts include: rock, clay, silt, sand, and humus are components of soils. (Science 3.7)
- The student will investigate and understand basic patterns and cycles occurring in nature. Key concepts include: animal life cycles. (Science 3.8)

Vocabulary: Clay, Kiln, Shape, Texture, Pattern, Ceramics, Bisque, Ceramic Glaze, and Line

Materials: -Clay -Clay tools -Water cups -9" x 12" Newspaper print -"Art smock"
   -Clay Glaze -Paintbrushes

Procedure:

1) Discuss as a class where clay comes from and the profession of a ceramicist.
2) Other topics to review: Where have students seen this type of artwork? Inception of this type of art? Uses throughout history? Have there been changes in pottery styles of today versus years past? How has this medium been affected by historic events?
3) Discuss personal interests and possible designs added to clay creations.
4) Discuss what we are making and the procedures/process.
5) They are given an "art smock" to wear during the activity.
6) Students will pick up the clay that has been placed on their newsprint paper, twist and break it into two pieces and place it back down on the paper.

 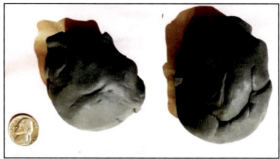

7) Students will pick up the largest piece out of the two and twist and break and place down on paper.

8) Students will pick up the largest piece out of the three and twist and break and place down on paper. Students will pick up the largest piece out of the four and pinch off a dime-sized piece. Separate this piece into two parts.

9) Students will pick up the largest two pieces. Taking one at a time, roll the piece of clay into a ball and flatten like a small pancake. Use the water to dip fingertips in and smooth out any cracks in the clay.

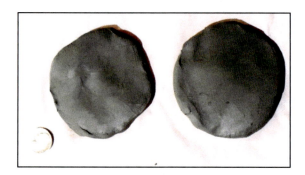

10) Students will press these two "pancakes" together with one side left open for the fish/shark mouth. Make sure the sides have been smoothed together.

11) The remaining largest 2 clay pieces are pressed into two more "pancake" shapes.

12) The two "pancake" shapes are cut into either half circles or triangles depending whether student is creating a fish or a shark.

Fish Fins **Shark Fins**

13) These fins are attached to each side of fish/shark and on top as the dorsal fin. Make sure to use fingers to smooth each fin into the body of the creature. Small drops of water may assist in this blending process.

14) Eyes are attached. Using clay tools, pattern is added. Teeth may be added to the shark.

 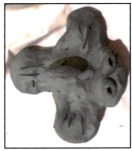 

15) When they are finished creating their fish/shark they are to write their initials and classroom teacher/grade on the bottom of the fish/shark.
16) After the fish/shark has dried and is bisque fired, students will paint their clay work using clay glaze. (They are also able to add pattern with the colored glazes.) The artwork is complete after the final stage of ceramic firing.
17) When projects are complete, students discuss among tablemates their choices of color and design. They will compare and contrast how each student's work is aesthetically different and that is a celebrated feature of art.

**Recommended student reading:

The Magic of Clay by Adalucia

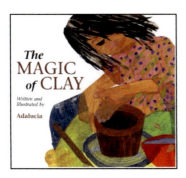

**Recommended student video:

Crystal Productions CP5267 *Dropping In on...Puffer-Ceramics* DVD

Assessment:

Teacher uses a range of formal and informal assessment strategies to gain insight into students' understanding of lesson, goal achievement, and progress.

Informal:

- Students participate in a class discussion during which questions outlined at the beginning of the lesson are reviewed.
- Individual student-teacher conferences take place during which teacher circulates around classroom assisting students with art project and offering guidance to any questions.
- Teacher observes student work to determine if they used art materials correctly and if they creatively apply skills learned.
- Students participate in a class critique.

Formal:

- Students complete a self-assessment worksheet written in kid-friendly language.
- Teacher completes rubric and uses the tool to evaluate student progress.

**Sample Assessment sheets are located in the book *Appendix*.

Science: Skeleton Action Figure

Objectives: 3rd Grade

- The student will identify innovative solutions used by artists to solve art-making problems. (Visual Art 3.1)
- The student will use imaginative and expressive strategies to create works of art. (Visual Art 3.4)
- The student will create works of art that communicate ideas, themes, and feelings. (Visual Art 3.6)
- The student will use the following in works of art: Balance—symmetry, asymmetry, radial. (Visual Art 3.7)
- The student will analyze personal works of art, using elements of art and principles of design. (Visual Art 3.19)
- The student will express informed judgments about works of art. (Visual Art 3.20)
- The student will demonstrate an understanding of scientific reasoning, logic, and the nature of science by planning and conducting investigations in which: models are designed and built; and current applications are used to reinforce science concepts. (Science 3.1)

Vocabulary: Skeleton bones, Balance, Symmetry, and Line

Materials: -8.5" x 11.5" Black construction paper -9" x 12" Colored construction paper -Construction paper crayons -Glue -Cotton swabs -Scissors -Black "Sharpie"

Procedure:

1) Discuss personal interests and possible designs added to skeletal creations.
2) Discuss what we are making and the procedures/process.
3) Review skeletal system and name of bones.

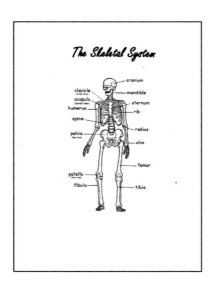

4) Discuss possible actions/movements students may show their figure doing. Ex) running, skating, dancing, etc.
5) Students arrange cotton swabs (without gluing on black paper). Swabs may be cut.
6) Once satisfied with placement of swabs, glue onto paper.
7) Once dry, add features to figure with construction paper crayons. Ex) head, hands, shoes, clothing, etc.
8) Label their action (i.e. Running, Dancing, etc.) and choose colored construction paper for boarder.
9) Add design/pattern around boarder in black "Sharpie."
10) Students discuss among tablemates their choices of color and design. They will compare and contrast how each student's work is aesthetically different and that is a celebrated feature of art.

<u>**Recommended Student Reading</u>:

The Skeleton Inside You (Let's Read-and-Find-Out Science 2) by Philip Balestrino

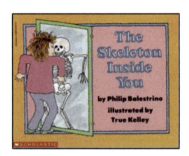

**Recommended student videos:

(Getting To Know) The Elements of Art

**Recommended artwork for lesson demonstration:

 Vincent van Gogh. *Skeleton.* 1886. Pencil on paper. Van Gogh Museum, Amsterdam, Netherlands.

Assessment:

Teacher uses a range of formal and informal assessment strategies to gain insight into students' understanding of lesson, goal achievement, and progress.

Informal:

- Students participate in a class discussion during which questions outlined at the beginning of the lesson are reviewed.
- Individual student-teacher conferences take place during which teacher circulates around classroom assisting students with art project and offering guidance to any questions.

- Teacher observes student work to determine if they used art materials correctly and if they creatively apply skills learned.
- Students participate in a class critique.

<u>Formal:</u>

- Students complete a self-assessment worksheet written in kid-friendly language.
- Teacher completes rubric and uses the tool to evaluate student progress.

**Sample Assessment sheets are located in the book *Appendix*.

Science: Animals in their Habitat Printmaking

Objectives: 4th Grade

- The student will use steps of the art making process, including brainstorming, preliminary sketching, planning, and reflecting, to generate ideas for and create works of art. (Visual Art 4.1)
- The student will demonstrate craftsmanship in personal works of art. (Visual Art 4.2)
- The student will use imaginative and expressive imagery to create works of art. (Visual Art 4.3)
- The student will make artistic choices to create compositional unity in works of art. (Visual Art 4.7)
- The student will identify ways that works of art from popular culture reflect the past and influence the present. (Visual Art 4.16)
- The student will analyze works of art based on visual properties and contextual information. (Visual Art 4.18)
- The student will formulate questions about aesthetic aspects of works of art. (Visual Art 4.21)
- The student will explain preferences for works of art by responding to aesthetic questions. (Visual Art 4.23)
- The student will investigate and understand basic plant anatomy and life processes. (Science 4.4)
- The student will investigate and understand how plants and animals, including humans, in an ecosystem interact with one another and with the nonliving components in the ecosystem. (Science 4.5)

Vocabulary: Printmaking, Monoprint, Line, Design, Habitat, Wildlife, and Repetition

Materials: -6" x 9" Rough draft paper -*How to Draw* books -6" x 9" Foam board ("Scratchfoam") -Brayer -Etching stick -Printing inks -Tray for ink -Markers -Construction paper (matting) -Masking tape

Procedure:

1) Discuss as a class the technique of printmaking and show examples. Explain there are many types of printmaking techniques including: linocut, woodcut, etching, engraving, monotype, lithography, screen print, digital print, and transfer.
2) Other topics to review: Where have students seen this type of artwork? Inception of this type of art? Uses throughout history? Have there been changes in printmaking styles of today versus years past?
3) Discuss what we are making and the procedures/process.
4) Students choose animal generated from class discussion about animals and their habitats.
5) Students practice on 6" x 9" rough draft paper drawing creature. "How to Draw" books may be used for ideas.
6) Once teacher has approved the rough draft picture, the student will trace over it with "Sharpie."

7) Students will use paper that the animal is on and tape it to a 6" x 9" foam board.

8) Using a wooden "etching stick" students go over (trace) the drawing (leaving an indention in the foam board.)
9) When complete the student will remove the practice paper. Students add final details to the foam board.
10) After teacher approval, the student will choose a color of printing ink. Students will also choose the color of their printmaking paper.
11) Students take a Styrofoam tray and squirt ink onto the top edge of the tray.
12) In order to spread out the ink, student uses a brayer and rolls the ink out in the tray.
13) Place the foam board onto a clean tray face up (designed side facing upward). Roll the ink-covered brayer over the design. Try not to allow the ink to get into the grooves of the drawing.
14) After the foam board is coated with ink take the "etching stick" and scrap out any paint that has gotten into the design crevices. (Because these lines will not show up in the printed design.)
15) Once the student is satisfied with their foam board they may take the ink-coated foam and place it (designed side down) in the center of the printmaking paper.
16) Once the work dries, the student may draw designs around the boarder of the ink-print and mat with cut paper.
17) Students discuss among tablemates their choices of color and design. They will compare and contrast how each student's work is aesthetically different and that is a celebrated feature of art.

Recommended student reading:

Frida Kahlo and Her Animalitos by Monica Brown

Dropping in on Rousseau by Pamela Geiger Stephens

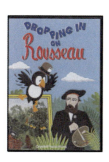

**Recommended student videos:

Printmaking Basis Techniques by Peggy Flores (Crystal Productions)

Printmaking: Introduce Students to the Ease and Fun of Basic Printmaking by Crystal Productions

**Recommended artwork for lesson demonstration:

Henri de Toulouse-Lautrec. *Jane Avril.* 1893. 130 x 95 cm. Private Collection.

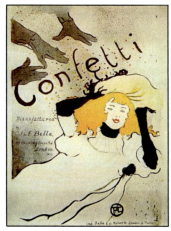 Henri de Toulouse-Lautrec. *Confetti*. 1894. 54.5 x 38 cm. Private Collection.

 Katsushika Hokusai. *A Colored Version of the Big Wave*.

 Hiroshige. *Drum Bridge and Setting Sun Hill, Meguro*. 1858. Private Collection.

Assessment:

Teacher uses a range of formal and informal assessment strategies to gain insight into students' understanding of lesson, goal achievement, and progress.

Informal:

- Students participate in a class discussion during which questions outlined at the beginning of the lesson are reviewed.
- Individual student-teacher conferences take place during which teacher circulates around classroom assisting students with art project and offering guidance to any questions.
- Teacher observes student work to determine if they used art materials correctly and if they creatively apply skills learned.
- Students participate in a class critique.

Formal:

- Students complete a self-assessment worksheet written in kid-friendly language.
- Teacher completes rubric and uses the tool to evaluate student progress.

**Sample Assessment sheets are located in the book *Appendix*.

Science: Clay Leaves

Objectives: Grade 4

- The student will create works of art that connect ideas, art forms, or cultural themes to personal experiences. (Visual Art 4.4)
- The student will make artistic choices to create compositional unity in works of art. (Visual Art 4.7)
- The student will describe and use hand-building techniques to make a ceramic work of art. (Visual Art 4.10)
- The student will describe the roles of crafts and artisans in various cultures. (Visual Art 4.12)
- The student will analyze works of art based on visual properties and contextual information. (Visual Art 4.18)
- The student will formulate questions about aesthetic aspects of works of art. (Visual Art 4.21)
- The student will explain preferences for works of art by responding to aesthetic questions. (Visual Art 4.23)
- The student will investigate and understand basic plant anatomy and life processes. Key concepts include: the structures of typical plants and the function of each structure; photosynthesis; and adaptations allow plants to satisfy life needs and respond to the environment. (Science 4.4)
- The student will investigate and understand important Virginia natural resources. Key concepts include: plants. (Science 4.9)

Vocabulary: Clay, Kiln, Shape, Texture, Pattern, Photosynthesis, Imprint, Wedging, Ceramics, Bisque, Ceramic Glaze, Clay Slab, and Line

Materials: -Clay -Clay tools -Water cups -Newsprint (9" x 12") -Rolling pin -Paint brush -"Art smock" -Fresh Leaves* -Wooden sticks -Cooking spray -1/2 of Styrofoam ball -Clay Glaze

Procedure:

1) Discuss as a class where clay comes from and the profession of a ceramicist.
2) Other topics to review: Where have students seen this type of artwork? Inception of this type of art? Uses throughout history? Have there been changes in pottery styles of today versus years past? How has this medium been affected by historic events?
3) Discuss leaf color change (photosynthesis) and what causes it in the fall.
4) Students are given real leaves (about the size of a hand) to choose from (The variety varies depending on geographical location.) Ex) Tulip Poplar, Maple, etc.
5) Discuss what we are making and the procedures/process.
6) Students are given an "art smock" to wear during the activity.
7) Students will pick up the clay that has been placed on their newsprint flatten with their hands in the air. Once it is somewhat flattened, they place it back on their paper and use

a rolling pin to roll out a flat surface. It will be about as thick as a pancake. (Wedging to get out air bubbles. Students are creating a clay slab.)

8) Place the leaf onto the middle of the rolled out clay. Take the rolling pin and roll over the leaf. This will imprint the clay image/veins into the clay.
9) Take the pointed part of the wooden stick and use it to cut out the leaf along the outside lines of the leaf.
10) Students put the extra clay aside.
11) They pick up the ½ Styrofoam ball with the round side up and spray it with the cooking spray.
12) Place the cutout leaf onto the ball (vein side down).
13) Gently press onto the leaf so it conforms to the ball shape.
14) Use the wooden stick to write initials and year into the clay.
15) Place the leaf/ball onto a tray for drying.
16) After the leaf has been bisque fired, student will paint the leaves using fall colors or special clay glazes.
17) When projects are complete, students discuss among tablemates their choices of color and design. They will compare and contrast how each student's work is aesthetically different and that is a celebrated feature of art.

*In a pinch, could use plastic leaf rubbings instead of real leaves.

**Recommended student reading:

Clay Boy by Mirra Ginsburg

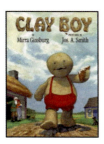

The Magic of Clay by Adalucia

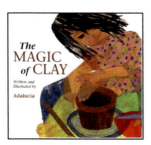

**Recommended student video:

Dropping In on Puffer…Learns about Ceramics by Crystal Production

Assessment:

Teacher uses a range of formal and informal assessment strategies to gain insight into students' understanding of lesson, goal achievement, and progress.

Informal:

- Students participate in a class discussion during which questions outlined at the beginning of the lesson are reviewed.

- Individual student-teacher conferences take place during which teacher circulates around classroom assisting students with art project and offering guidance to any questions.
- Teacher observes student work to determine if they used art materials correctly and if they creatively apply skills learned.
- Students participate in a class critique.

Formal:

- Students complete a self-assessment worksheet written in kid-friendly language.
- Teacher completes rubric and uses the tool to evaluate student progress.

**Sample Assessment sheets are located in the book *Appendix*.

Science: Georgia O'Keeffe Inspired Oil Pastel Flowers

Objectives: 5th Grade

- The student will use steps of the art making process, including brainstorming, preliminary sketching, planning, reflecting, and refining, to synthesize ideas for and create works of art. (Visual Art 5.1)
- The student will execute and complete works of art with attention to detail and craftsmanship. (Visual Art 5.2)
- The student will express personal ideas, images, and themes through artistic choices of media, techniques, and subject matter. (Visual Art 5.3)
- The student will identify and apply ethical decisions in art making. (Visual Art 5.4)
- The student will use the following to express meaning in works of art: Color—student-mixed hues, tints, shades, tones; Texture—surface embellishment; Value—gradation to create the illusion of depth on a two-dimensional surface; Balance—formal, informal. (Visual Art 5.5)
- The student will use size and proportion to emphasize spatial relationships in works of art. (Visual Art 5.7)
- The student will investigate and understand that organisms are made of one or more cells and have distinguishing characteristics that play a vital role in the organism's ability to survive and thrive in its environment. Key concepts include: basic cell structures and functions; classification of organisms using physical characteristics, body structures, and behavior of the organism; and traits of organisms that allow them to survive in their environment. (Science 5.5)
- The student will analyze and interpret works of art based on visual properties and context. (Visual Art 5.18)
- The student will analyze an artist's point of view based on contextual information. (Visual Art 5.19)
- The student will use specific criteria to evaluate a finished product. (Visual Art 5.20)
- The student will compare and contrast objects in terms of aesthetic preferences. (Visual Art 5.23)
- The student will reflect on and describe the nature of art. (Visual Art 5.24)

Vocabulary: Microscopic, Blending, Shading, Texture, Color, Composition, Balance, Line and Design

Materials: -14" x 14" Black construction paper -15" x 15" Colored construction paper (matting) -16" x 16" Colored construction paper (matting) -18" x 18" Black construction paper (matting) -Oil pastels -Pencil -Scratch paper -Glitter glue -Black glue

Procedure:

1) After discussing O'Keeffe's style of flowers paintings, students practice drawing their own on practice paper. (Petals should go off the page. If student includes the center of

flower, is should be drawn off center. Flowers are drawn from a microscopic perspective.)

  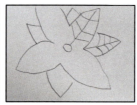 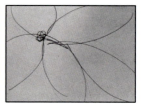

2) Using a 14" x 14" piece of black paper, draw a flower in pencil.
3) With oil pastels, color in the petals. (May use blending and shading techniques.)

4) Let dry (a day). Repeat step 3 for depth/vibrancy.
5) This step is optional. May outline the petals/edges of flower/stems/leaves with black glue or glitter glue.
6) When dry, students may mat artwork.
7) Students discuss among tablemates their choices of color and design. They will compare and contrast how each student's work is aesthetically different and that is a celebrated feature of art.

Recommended student reading:

Georgia O'Keeffe (Getting to Know the World's Greatest Artists) by Mike Venezia

Through Georgia's Eyes by Rachel Rodríguez

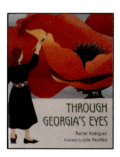

**Recommended student videos:

Elements and Principles of Design by Crystal Productions

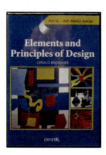

**Recommended artwork for lesson demonstration:

Georgia O'Keeffe. *Inside Red Canna.* 1919.

Georgia O'Keeffe. *Series I, No. 8.* 1918.

Georgia O'Keeffe. *Canna Red and Orange*. 1922

Assessment:

Teacher uses a range of formal and informal assessment strategies to gain insight into students' understanding of lesson, goal achievement, and progress.

Informal:

- Students participate in a class discussion during which questions outlined at the beginning of the lesson are reviewed.
- Individual student-teacher conferences take place during which teacher circulates around classroom assisting students with art project and offering guidance to any questions.
- Teacher observes student work to determine if they used art materials correctly and if they creatively apply skills learned.
- Students participate in a class critique.

Formal:

- Students complete a self-assessment worksheet written in kid-friendly language.
- Teacher completes rubric and uses the tool to evaluate student progress.

**Sample Assessment sheets are located in the book *Appendix*.

Science: Pointillism

Objectives: 5th Grade

- The student will use steps of the art making process, including brainstorming, preliminary sketching, planning, reflecting, and refining, to synthesize ideas for and create works of art. (Visual Art 5.1)
- The student will execute and complete works of art with attention to detail and craftsmanship. (Visual Art 5.2)
- The student will identify and apply ethical decisions in art making. (Visual Art 5.4)
- The student will use the following to express meaning in works of art: Color—student-mixed hues, tints, shades, tones; Value—gradation to create the illusion of depth on a two-dimensional surface; Balance—formal, informal. (Visual Art 5.5)
- The student will use size and proportion to emphasize spatial relationships in works of art. (Visual Art 5.7)
- The student will analyze and interpret works of art based on visual properties and context. (Visual Art 5.18)
- The student will analyze an artist's point of view based on contextual information. (Visual Art 5.19)
- The student will use specific criteria to evaluate a finished product. (Visual Art 5.20)
- The student will compare and contrast objects in terms of aesthetic preferences. (Visual Art 5.23)
- The student will reflect on and describe the nature of art. (Visual Art 5.24)
- The student will investigate and understand that organisms are made of one or more cells and have distinguishing characteristics that play a vital role in the organism's ability to survive and thrive in its environment. Key concepts include: basic cell structures and functions; classification of organisms using physical characteristics, body structures, and behavior of the organism; and traits of organisms that allow them to survive in their environment. (Science 5.5)

Vocabulary: Color Theory, Color, Line, Shapes, Shading, Highlighting, Vertical, Horizontal, and Neo-Impressionism

Materials: -Scratch paper -Pencil -Black "Sharpie" -Watercolors -Metallic Watercolors -Eraser -Cotton swabs -Water cups -11" x 11" Watercolor paper -12" x 12" Colored construction paper (matting) -13" x 13" Colored construction paper (matting) -15" x 15" black construction paper (matting)

Procedure:

1) After discussing color theory and the art technique that Georges Seurat developed—Pointillism, students practice drawing an item (large) in nature (flower, animal, insect, etc.) on practice paper.
2) Discuss what we are making and the procedures/process.
3) Student uses a pencil to draw their item on watercolor paper.
4) They trace over the pencil marks with black "Sharpie."

5) Erase pencil marks.
6) Keeping in mind the techniques of shading and highlighting, student chooses a darker shade of watercolor for the edges of the item. Using increasingly lighter tones, they gradually move into center of artwork. All of this is done with the technique of pointillism—using a cotton swab. All dots are close together in the same manner of Seurat with the thought the eye will blend the color.

7) After the central figure is completed and painted, the negative space around the object should reflect the habitat of the creature. Drawn first with pencil, then traced over with black "Sharpie." Paint this area in the Pointillist style.
8) The remaining space is also dotted in the Pointillist style.
9) When dry, artwork is matted with colored construction paper. Black is used last.
10) Students discuss among tablemates their choices of color and design. They will compare and contrast how each student's work is aesthetically different and that is a celebrated feature of art.

**<u>Recommended student reading</u>:

George Seurat by Mike Venezia   *The Life and Work of…George Seurat* by Paul Flux

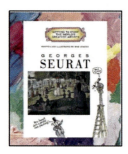   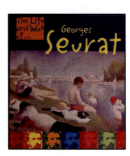

A Book About Color: A Clear and Simple Guide for Young Artists by Mark Gonyea

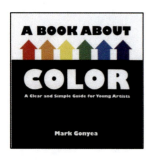

Mix It Up! by Herve Tullet

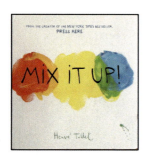

**<u>Recommended student videos</u>:

Color by Crystal Productions

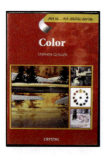

**Recommended artwork for lesson demonstration:

Georges Seurat. *Sunday Afternoon on the Island of La Grande Jatte*. 1884-1886. Pointillism. Oil on canvas. 207.5 x 308 cm. Art Institute of Chicago, Chicago, Illinois.

Georges Seurat. *Circus Sideshow*. 1887-1888. Pointillism. Oil on canvas. 100 x 155.5 cm. Metropolitan Museum of Art, New York City, New York.

Georges Seurat. *Chahut*. 1889-1890. Oil on canvas. 169 x 141 cm. Kröller-Müller Museum, Otterlo, Netherlands

 Georges Seurat. *The Eiffel Tower.* 1889. Oil on wood. 24 x 15 cm. Fine Arts Museum of San Francisco, San Francisco, California.

Assessment:

Teacher uses a range of formal and informal assessment strategies to gain insight into students' understanding of lesson, goal achievement, and progress.

Informal:

- Students participate in a class discussion during which questions outlined at the beginning of the lesson are reviewed.
- Individual student-teacher conferences take place during which teacher circulates around classroom assisting students with art project and offering guidance to any questions.
- Teacher observes student work to determine if they used art materials correctly and if they creatively apply skills learned.
- Students participate in a class critique.

Formal:

- Students complete a self-assessment worksheet written in kid-friendly language.
- Teacher completes rubric and uses the tool to evaluate student progress.

**Sample Assessment sheets are located in the book *Appendix*.

2 TECHNOLOGY + ART

Technology: Color Theory

Objectives: 3rd Grade

- The student will express informed judgments about works of art. (Visual Art 3.20)
- The student will develop ideas inspired by a variety of sources, including print, nonprint, and contemporary media, for incorporation into works of art. (Visual Art 3.5)
- The student will analyze personal works of art, using elements of art and principles of design. (Visual Art 3.19)
- The student will express informed judgments about works of art. (Visual Art 3.20)
- Identify and use available technologies to complete specific tasks (Computer Technology 3-5.2)
- Demonstrate digital citizenship by actively participating in positive activities for personal and community well-being. (Computer Technology 3-5.5)
- Communicate effectively with others (e.g., peers, teachers, experts) in collaborative learning situations. (Computer Technology 3-5.10)

Vocabulary: Color Theory, Primary Colors, Secondary Colors, Color Wheel, Warm Colors, Cool Colors, Complementary Colors, and Intermediate Colors

Materials: -*Smartboard* -*Smartboard* tools ("wand") -Computer -Color Wheel -Colors *Smartboard* software -9" x 12" White construction paper -Markers

Procedure:

1) Discuss as a class colors. What are the primary colors? What are the secondary colors?
2) Explain warm, cool, complementary colors, and intermediate colors.
3) Students take turns interacting with *Smartboard* technology and website (below) to recall colors and the categories they are under.
4) When one student is finished, they choose a classmate to come to the board. This process continues until every child has the opportunity to participate.
5) At the end of the lesson the class discusses with their tablemates: a) when in nature these colors are found? b) when in their surroundings they find these colors?
6) Students may draw a picture using one of the color groups they learned about. Ex) A picture using only warm colors. Students discuss among tablemates their choices of color and design. Students will compare and contrast how each student's work is aesthetically different and that is a celebrated feature of art.

**Websites for Smartboard interaction:

- http://express.smarttech.com/?url=http://exchangedownloads.smarttech.com/public/content/20/20a11e8e-4b6f-4563-ad8f-b283d93f5db9/Color%20theory.notebook#

- https://prezi.com/xzpo1dvrklir/beginning-color-theory/

- http://www.artyfactory.com/color_theory/color_terms_1.htm

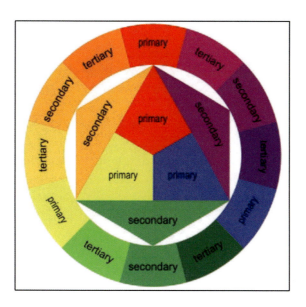

*Also known as Tertiary colors.

Recommended student reading:

Mix it Up! by Herve Tullet

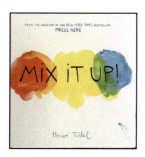

Recommended student videos:

Color by Crystal Productions *(Getting To Know) The Elements of Art*

Assessment:

Teacher uses a range of formal and informal assessment strategies to gain insight into students' understanding of lesson, goal achievement, and progress.

Informal:

- Students participate in a class discussion during which questions outlined at the beginning of the lesson are reviewed.
- Individual student-teacher conferences take place during which teacher circulates around classroom assisting students with art project and offering guidance to any questions.
- Teacher observes student work to determine if they used art materials correctly and if they creatively apply skills learned.
- Students participate in a class critique.

Formal:

- Students complete a self-assessment worksheet written in kid-friendly language.
- Teacher completes rubric and uses the tool to evaluate student progress.

**Sample Assessment sheets are located in the book *Appendix*.

Technology: Research Artist and Art History

Objectives: 4th Grade

- The student will describe the roles of crafts and artisans in various cultures. (Visual Art 4.12)
- The student will describe artists and their work. (Visual Art 4.13)
- The student will identify a variety of artists and art careers. (Visual Art 4.15)
- The student will analyze works of art based on visual properties and contextual information. (Visual Art 4.18)
- The student will formulate questions about aesthetic aspects of works of art. (Visual Art 4.21)
- The student will explain preferences for works of art by responding to aesthetic questions. (Visual Art 4.23)
- Demonstrate an operational knowledge of various technologies. (Computer Technology 3-5.1)
- Identify and use available technologies to complete specific tasks. (Computer Technology 3-5.2)
- Demonstrate digital citizenship by actively participating in positive activities for personal and community well being. (Computer Technology 3-5.5)
- Plan and apply strategies for gathering information, using a variety of tools and sources, and reflect on alternate strategies that might lead to greater successes in future projects. (Computer Technology 3-5.6)
- Draw conclusions from research and relate these findings to real-world situations. (Computer Technology 3-5.7)
- Practice reasoning skills when gathering and evaluating data. (Computer Technology 3-5.8)
- Communicate effectively with others (e.g., peers, teachers, experts) in collaborative learning situations. (Computer Technology 3-5.10)

Vocabulary: Art History, *Microsoft PowerPoint* software, and Research

Materials: -Computer Lab -PowerPoint software -Printer Paper -Printer

Procedure:

1) Discuss as a class: "What is art history?"
2) Discuss as a class how we research artists, their style of art, their lives, and appropriate websites to use.
3) Students choose an artist that interests them. Get teacher approval.
4) Students research artists in the computer lab and generate a *Microsoft PowerPoint* to share with the class form their findings.
5) Students print out *PowerPoint* (after making corrections).
6) Students take turns presenting their projects to the class. They may dress up as their artists.
7) Other students are encouraged to ask questions to the presenter.

8) When one student is finished, they choose a classmate to come to the front of class. This process continues until every child has the opportunity to participate.

Recommended student reading:

Child's Introduction to Art: The World's Greatest Paintings and Sculptures by Heather Alexander

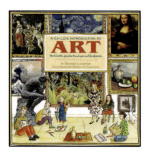

The Art Book for Children by Editors of Phaidon Press

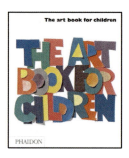

Children's Book of Art by DK Publishing

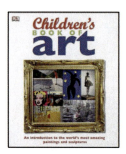

Recommended student video:

Arts and Technology: https://jr.brainpop.com

Assessment:

Teacher uses a range of formal and informal assessment strategies to gain insight into students' understanding of lesson, goal achievement, and progress.

Informal:

- Students participate in a class discussion during which questions outlined at the beginning of the lesson are reviewed.
- Individual student-teacher conferences take place during which teacher circulates around classroom assisting students with art project and offering guidance to any questions.
- Teacher observes student work to determine if they used art materials correctly and if they creatively apply skills learned.
- Students participate in a class critique.

Formal:

- Students complete a self-assessment worksheet written in kid-friendly language.
- Teacher completes rubric and uses the tool to evaluate student progress.

**Sample Assessment sheets are located in the book *Appendix*.

Technology: 1-Point Perspective

Objectives: 5th Grade

- The student will use steps of the art making process, including brainstorming, preliminary sketching, planning, reflecting, and refining, to synthesize ideas for and create works of art. (Visual Art 5.1)
- The student will execute and complete works of art with attention to detail and craftsmanship. (Visual Art 5.2)
- The student will identify and apply ethical decisions in art making. (Visual Art 5.4)
- The student will use the following to express meaning in works of art: Color—student-mixed hues, tints, shades, tones; Value—gradation to create the illusion of depth on a two-dimensional surface; Balance—formal, informal. (Visual Art 5.5)
- The student will use atmospheric perspective in works of art. (Visual Art 5.6)
- The student will use size and proportion to emphasize spatial relationships in works of art. (Visual Art 5.7)
- The student will analyze and interpret works of art based on visual properties and context. (Visual Art 5.18)
- The student will use specific criteria to evaluate a finished product. (Visual Art 5.20)
- Identify and use available technologies to complete specific tasks. (Computer Technology 3-5.2)
- Exhibit personal responsibility for appropriate, legal, and ethical conduct. (Computer Technology 3-5.4)
- Use models and simulations to understand complex systems and processes. (Computer Technology 3-5.9)

Vocabulary: Linear Perspective/1-point perspective, 3-Dimensional, 2-Dimensional, Vanishing Point, Horizon Line, Orthogonal, Vertical, and Interior

Materials: -Computer Lab -Google "Sketch-Up" -Typing Paper -Printer -Pencil -Website: https://www.sketchup.com -Drawing Paper -Ruler

Procedure:

1) Discuss as a class the concept of 1-pt. perspective.
2) Questions to discuss: Where have students seen this type of artwork? Uses throughout history? How has this medium been affected by historic events?
3) Discuss foreground, middle ground, background, vanishing point, and horizon line with students. Show examples of artwork detailing the technique.
4) Discuss personal interests and possible designs added to their 1-pt. perspective creations on the computer.
5) Discuss what we are making and the procedures/process.
6) Take students to computer lab where they will use "Google Sketch-Up"* to create their own interior room using 1-point perspective.
7) Next, they will create their own 1-point perspective drawing using the following steps:

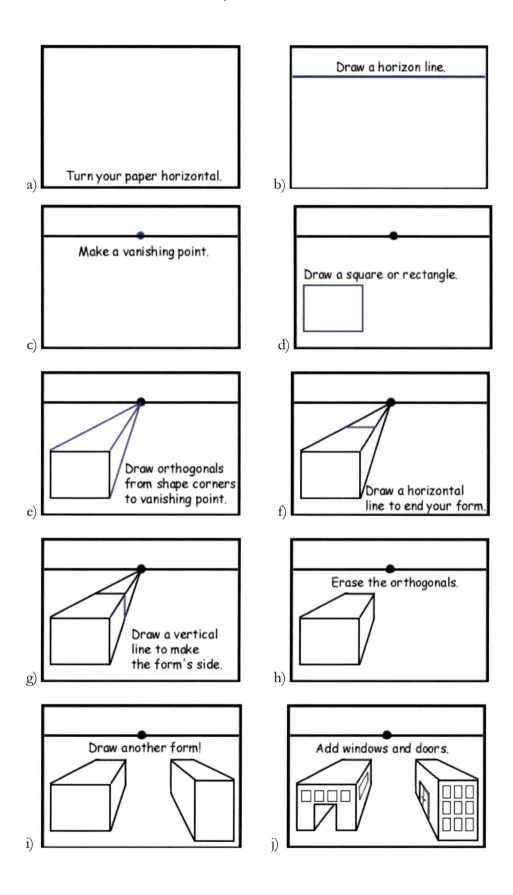

8) Students pick a partner in the lab and show one another their work. Together, they take turns discussing their choices of color and design. They will compare and contrast how each student's work is aesthetically different and that is a celebrated feature of art.

*Educators may get the program free with proof of required credentials. Please see website: https://www.sketchup.com/3Dfor/education-educators

<u>Recommended Student Reading</u>:

Iggy Peck, Architect by Andrea Beaty

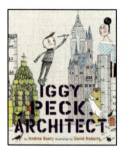

13 Architects Children Should Know by Florian Heine

<u>Recommended student videos</u>:

Elements and Principles of Design by Crystal Productions

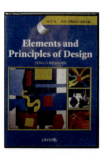

Recommended artwork for lesson demonstration:

- Giorgio de Chirico. *Italian Plaza with a Red Tower.* 1943. Oil on canvas.
- Giorgio de Chirico. *Italian Plaza with Equestrian Statue.* Oil on canvas.

Giorgio de Chirico. *Piazza d'Italia.* 1913. Oil on canvas. 35.2 x 26 cm. Art Gallery of Ontario (AGO), Toronto, Canada.

Assessment:

Teacher uses a range of formal and informal assessment strategies to gain insight into students' understanding of lesson, goal achievement, and progress.

Informal:

- Students participate in a class discussion during which questions outlined at the beginning of the lesson are reviewed.
- Individual student-teacher conferences take place during which teacher circulates around classroom assisting students with art project and offering guidance to any questions.
- Teacher observes student work to determine if they used art materials correctly and if they creatively apply skills learned.
- Students participate in a class critique.

Formal:

- Students complete a self-assessment worksheet written in kid-friendly language.
- Teacher completes rubric and uses the tool to evaluate student progress.

**Sample Assessment sheets are located in the book *Appendix*.

3 ENGINEERING + ART

Engineering: City Collage Based on Artwork of Romare Bearden

Objectives: 3rd Grade

- The student will identify innovative solutions used by artists to solve art-making problems. (Visual Art 3.1)
- The student will describe and use steps of the art making process, including brainstorming, preliminary sketching, and planning, to create works of art. (Visual Art 3.2)
- The student will use imaginative and expressive strategies to create works of art. (Visual Art 3.4)
- The student will develop ideas inspired by a variety of sources, including print, nonprint, and contemporary media, for incorporation into works of art. (Visual Art 3.5)
- The student will create works of art that communicate ideas, themes, and feelings. (Visual Art 3.6)
- The student will use the following in works of art: Balance—symmetry, asymmetry, radial. (Visual Art 3.7)
- The student will identify how works of art and craft reflect times, places, and cultures. (Visual Art 3.11)
- The student will identify how history, culture, and the visual arts influence each other. (Visual Art 3.13)
- The student will analyze personal works of art, using elements of art and principles of design. (Visual Art 3.19)
- The student will express informed judgments about works of art. (Visual Art 3.20)
- The student will develop and describe personal reasons for valuing works of art. (Visual Art 3.23)
- Student will design a community using elements of engineering (building and transportation). (Engineering)

Vocabulary: Collage, Jazz, Cityscapes, Overlap, and Rhythm

Materials: -Watercolors -Magazine images -11" x 17" White paper -Pencil. -Eraser -Visual examples -Music images -Black "Sharpie" -Jazz music

Procedure:

1) Review Romare Bearden, his art, and legacy. Discuss collage techniques. Aspects of Romare Bearden's art that are replicated in this lesson: emphasis on jazz music, city life, transportation, and cityscapes.
2) Discuss personal interests and possible designs added to collage creations.
3) Discuss what we are making and the procedures/process.
4) Students are provided with magazines and music images. It is helpful to play jazz in the background while students work.
5) Students glue down at least three people in their work. Students overlap their features with features from others to create interest. Ex) Add a face. Affix eyes from another

person. Affix a mouth from a different person. Ex) Place a head on another person's body.
6) Glue down musical instruments and cars.
7) Use pencil to add a road, picture frame, jazz instruments, lines for image separation, buildings, person's body, etc.

8) When white space has been filled, trace over pencil with black "Sharpie." Erase pencil marks.

9) Paint artwork with watercolor.
10) When dry, mat artwork.
11) Students discuss among tablemates their choices of color and design. They will compare and contrast how each student's work is aesthetically different and that is a celebrated feature of art.

<u>**Recommended student reading</u>:

Me and Uncle Romie: A Story Inspired by the Life and Art of Romare Bearden by Clarie Hartfield

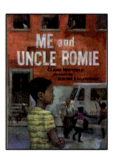

Recommended student videos:

The Art of Romare Bearden with Danny Glover (Actor), Morgan Freeman (Actor), and Carroll Moore (Director)

Dropping in on Romare Bearden Tom and Loretta Hubbard (Directors)

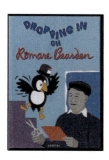

Recommended artwork for lesson demonstration:

- Romare Bearden. *The Block.* 1971. Mixed-Media Collage. 48" x 216" inches. The Metropolitan Museum of Art. Copyright © Romare Bearden Foundation/Licensed by VAGA, New York NY.

- Romare Bearden. *Prevalence of Ritual: Baptism.* 1964. Mixed Media Collage. $9 1/8$ x 12 inches. Hirshhorn Museum and Sculpture Garden, Smithsonian Institution.

- Romare Bearden. *Profile/Part II, The Thirties: Midtown Sunset.* 1981. Mixed Media Collage. 14 x 22 inches. Private Collection.

Assessment:

Teacher uses a range of formal and informal assessment strategies to gain insight into students' understanding of lesson, goal achievement, and progress.

Informal:

- Students participate in a class discussion during which questions outlined at the beginning of the lesson are reviewed.
- Individual student-teacher conferences take place during which teacher circulates around classroom assisting students with art project and offering guidance to any questions.
- Teacher observes student work to determine if they used art materials correctly and if they creatively apply skills learned.
- Students participate in a class critique.

Formal:

- Students complete a self-assessment worksheet written in kid-friendly language.
- Teacher completes rubric and uses the tool to evaluate student progress.

**Sample Assessment sheets are located in the book *Appendix*.

Engineering: Perspective Drawing

Objectives: 4th Grade

- The student will use steps of the art making process, including brainstorming, preliminary sketching, planning, and reflecting, to generate ideas for and create works of art. (Visual Art 4.1)
- The student will use imaginative and expressive imagery to create works of art. (Visual Art 4.3)
- The student will use the following to express meaning in works of art: Color: hue, tint, shade, intensity; Value: shading; Variety: to create interest. (Visual Art 4.5)
- The student will analyze how line choices affect the intent of a work of art and make selections accordingly. (Visual Art 4.6)
- The student will make artistic choices to create compositional unity in works of art. (Visual Art 4.7)
- The student will create the illusion of depth on a two-dimensional surface, using overlapping, size variation, and placement on the picture plane. (Visual Art 4.8)
- The student will use contour drawing and shading techniques to create observational drawings. (Visual Art 4.9)
- Student will design a community using elements of engineering (building and transportation). (Engineering)

Vocabulary: Foreground, Middle ground, Background, Vertical, Horizontal, Diagonal, Vanishing point, Horizon line, Shadowing, Highlighting, Line, Perspective, and Value

Materials: -11" x 17" White construction paper -Glue -Colored pencils -Pencil -Ruler -Colored construction paper (matting) -Eraser -Tortillions (shading)

Procedure:

1) Discuss as a class the concept of perspective drawing.
2) Questions to discuss: Where have students seen this type of artwork? Uses throughout history? How has this medium been affected by historic events?
3) Discuss foreground, middle ground, background, vanishing point, and horizon line with students. Show examples of artwork detailing the technique.
4) Discuss personal interests and possible designs added to 1-pt. perspective creations.
5) Discuss what we are making and the procedures/process.
6) Begin with a horizontal line across the length of the paper.
7) Place a dot in the center of this line. This is the vanishing point.

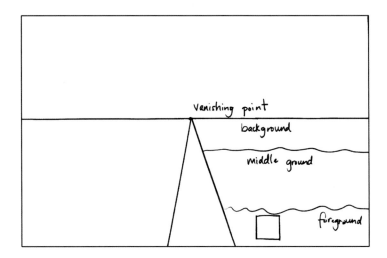

8) Draw two lines that begin at the vanishing point and extend off the paper. This could be a road, river, street, or railroad tracks.
9) For a house, start with a square. Draw a line to the vanishing point from the three closest corners of the square to the vanishing point.
10) Draw one vertical line (D) on this area to create the back corner of the house.
11) Draw an "X" in the square by connecting diagonal corners with a light pencil line.
12) Draw a vertical line straight up from the center of the "X." Draw it as tall as you want the peak of the roof to be.
13) Connect the top of this line (A) to the two top corners of the square (B &C).
14) Draw a line that connects from point (A) to the vanishing point. This will form the top of the roof.
15) Line your ruler up with points "A" & "B." Slide the ruler back at this same angle to point "D."

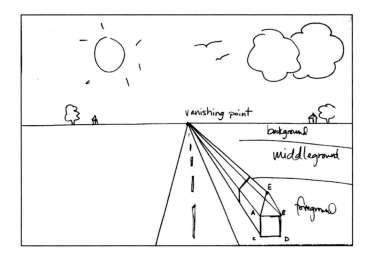

16) Erase all lines that start at the back edge of the house and extend to the vanishing point.
17) Try more buildings on either side of upside down "V".
18) Students will fill in items with colored pencils.

19) Students will learn and apply the technique of shadowing and highlighting using colored pencils.

20) Add more structures items to make the drawing complete (i.e. landscaping, roads, cars, lamp posts, animals, people, body of water, etc.)
21) When drawing is complete mat artwork.
22) Students discuss among tablemates their choices of color and design. They will compare and contrast how each student's work is aesthetically different and that is a celebrated feature of art.

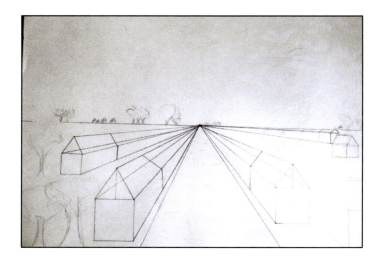

Recommended Student Reading:

Iggy Peck, Architect by Andrea Beaty

13 Architects Children Should Know by Florian Heine

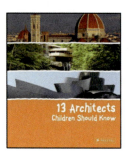

<u>Recommended student video</u>:

(Getting To Know) The Elements of Art

<u>Recommended artwork for lesson demonstration:</u>

 Gustave Caillebotte. *View of the Seine in the Direction of the Pont de Bezons.* 1892. Impressionism. Landscape. Oil. Private Collection.

Maurice Prendergast. *Charles Street, Boston.* 1895. Impressionism. Watercolor. 36.51 x 27.94 cm. Private Collection.

Hoca Ali Riza. *Manzara.* 1898. Impressionism.

Assessment:

Teacher uses a range of formal and informal assessment strategies to gain insight into students' understanding of lesson, goal achievement, and progress.

Informal:

- Students participate in a class discussion during which questions outlined at the beginning of the lesson are reviewed.
- Individual student-teacher conferences take place during which teacher circulates around classroom assisting students with art project and offering guidance to any questions.
- Teacher observes student work to determine if they used art materials correctly and if they creatively apply skills learned.
- Students participate in a class critique.

Formal:

- Students complete a self-assessment worksheet written in kid-friendly language.
- Teacher completes rubric and uses the tool to evaluate student progress.

**Sample Assessment sheets are located in the book *Appendix*.

Engineering: Cityscape Collage

Objectives: 5th Grade

- The student will execute and complete works of art with attention to detail and craftsmanship. (Visual Art 5.2)
- The student will express personal ideas, images, and themes through artistic choices of media, techniques, and subject matter. (Visual Art 5.3)
- The student will use size and proportion to emphasize spatial relationships in works of art. (Visual Art 5.7)
- Student will design a community using elements of engineering (building and transportation). (Engineering)

Vocabulary: Architecture, Cityscapes, Urban, Collage, Geometric, Balance, and Texture

Materials: -11" x17" black paper -12" x 18" Assorted colored paper (matting) -Ruler -10" x 3" x 16" Assorted cool colored construction paper (buildings) -Pencils -Scissors -Black "Sharpie" markers (windows) -Small yellow squares (windows) -Glue -3" x 3" Assorted colored construction paper (details)

Procedure:

1) Discuss as a class where the concept of collage originated and how artists use various materials to create collage—even everyday items like wall paint samples!
2) Other topics to review: Where have students seen this type of artwork? Uses throughout history? Have there been changes in collage styles of today versus years past? How has this medium been affected by historic events?
3) Discuss cityscapes and what we find in cities: architecture, transportation, streets, people, etc. Images of cities are shown to inspire.
4) Discuss personal interests and possible designs added to collage creations.
5) Discuss what we are making and the procedures/process.
6) Students learn about cityscapes and architecture.
7) Cityscape collages are created using textured paper and colored construction paper, with at least ten buildings created from geometric shapes. The buildings will overlap and go off the page.

8) Students add details to buildings. (i.e. windows)

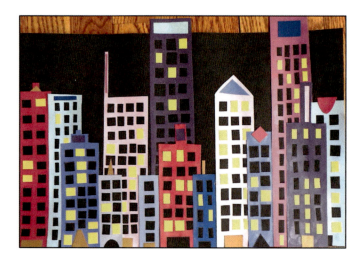

9) Students add objects to their city using collaged paper and glue. Possible details include: moon, stars, lamp posts, cars, street lights, street signs, etc.
10) Students are encouraged to brainstorm and add interesting items to their cityscape for uniqueness.
11) Completed artwork may be matted.

12) Students discuss among tablemates their choices of color and design. They will compare and contrast how each student's work is aesthetically different and that is a celebrated feature of art.

Recommended Student Reading:

Iggy Peck, Architect by Andrea Beaty

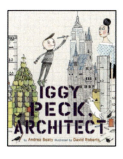

13 Architects Children Should Know by Florian Heine

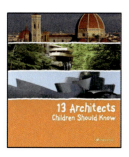

Recommended student videos:

Elements and Principles of Design by Crystal Productions

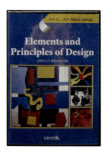

Recommended images for lesson demonstration:

Shanghai World Financial Center
Location: Shanghai, China
Photo courtesy of website: http://www.swfc-shanghai.com/?l=en

Two International Finance Centre
Location: Hong Kong, China

Chicago Skyline
Photo Courtesy of website: https://wikitravel.org/en/Chicago_skyline_guide

30 Rockefeller Plaza
Photo courtesy of website: https://en.wikipedia.org/wiki/30_Rockefeller_Plaza

Assessment:

Teacher uses a range of formal and informal assessment strategies to gain insight into students' understanding of lesson, goal achievement, and progress.

Informal:

- Students participate in a class discussion during which questions outlined at the beginning of the lesson are reviewed.
- Individual student-teacher conferences take place during which teacher circulates around classroom assisting students with art project and offering guidance to any questions.
- Teacher observes student work to determine if they used art materials correctly and if they creatively apply skills learned.
- Students participate in a class critique.

Formal:

- Students complete a self-assessment worksheet written in kid-friendly language.
- Teacher completes rubric and uses the tool to evaluate student progress.

**Sample Assessment sheets are located in the book *Appendix*.

4 MATHEMATICS + ART

Mathematics Pizza

Objectives: 3rd Grade

- The student will identify innovative solutions used by artists to solve art-making problems. (Visual Art 3.1)
- The student will create works of art that communicate ideas, themes, and feelings. (Visual Art 3.6)
- The student will analyze personal works of art, using elements of art and principles of design. (Visual Art 3.19)
- The student will express informed judgments about works of art. (Visual Art 3.20)
- The student will develop and describe personal reasons for valuing works of art. (Visual Art 3.23)
- The student will: name and write fractions (including mixed numbers) represented by a model; model fractions (including mixed numbers) and write the fractions' names. (Mathematics 3.3)

Vocabulary: Overlap, Shapes, Repetition, Fractions, and Line

Materials: -Pizza template (15.5" x 16" x 13") -12" x 18" Construction paper (Tan, brown, and orange) -3" x 3", 4" x 4", 5" x 5", and 6" x 6" Assorted colored construction paper (toppings) -3" x 18" Brown bulletin board paper (crust) -Markers -Scissors -13" x 13" Red construction paper (sauce) -Glue

Procedure:

1) Discuss fractions using entire piece of pizza. Divide pizza into sections using fractions. Read *Pizza Counting* by Christina Dobson to illustrate math concepts.
2) Choose paper for pizza and trace template.

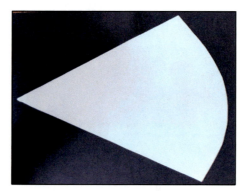

3) Cut out.
4) Brainstorm items that can be on pizza—Sweet or savory. Toppings drawn large for visibility.
5) Take four pieces of the same color of paper and create 1st topping for pizza.

6) Arrange on pizza and glue.
7) Repeat steps #5 and #6 with a different color choice. Overlap 2nd topping when gluing down onto pizza.
8) Repeat step #7 for a 3rd topping.
9) May add sauce by taking red paper and cutting curvy line out of one side of it. Glue down and cut off any remaining edges going off of pizza.

10) Use marker to add pattern and design to toppings. (Use same color of marker as paper embellishing.)
11) Twist brown paper for crust. **Teacher** glues on curst with glue gun.

12) Student may cut out 1-2 bites from pizza.
13) Tablemates use the time after pizza creation to combine their artwork to create fractions and discuss. Students discuss among tablemates their choices of color and design. They will compare and contrast how each student's work is aesthetically different and that is a celebrated feature of art.

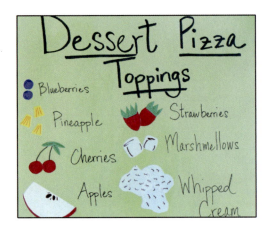 

**Suggested Student Reading:

Pizza Counting by Christina Dobson

**Recommended student videos:

Color by Crystal Productions

Assessment:

Teacher uses a range of formal and informal assessment strategies to gain insight into students' understanding of lesson, goal achievement, and progress.

Informal:

- Students participate in a class discussion during which questions outlined at the beginning of the lesson are reviewed.
- Individual student-teacher conferences take place during which teacher circulates around classroom assisting students with art project and offering guidance to any questions.
- Teacher observes student work to determine if they used art materials correctly and if they creatively apply skills learned.
- Students participate in a class critique.

Formal:

- Students complete a self-assessment worksheet written in kid-friendly language.
- Teacher completes rubric and uses the tool to evaluate student progress.

**Sample Assessment sheets are located in the book *Appendix*.

Mathematics: Vertical, Horizontal, and Diagonal Line Design

Objectives: 4th Grade

- The student will use the following to express meaning in works of art: Variety—to create interest. (Visual Art 4.5)
- The student will analyze how line choices affect the intent of a work of art and make selections accordingly. (Visual Art 4.6)
- The student will make artistic choices to create compositional unity in works of art. (Visual Art 4.7)
- The student will create the illusion of depth on a two-dimensional surface, using overlapping, size variation, and placement on the picture plane. (Visual Art 4.8)
- The student will analyze works of art based on visual properties and contextual information. (Visual Art 4.18)
- The student will formulate questions about aesthetic aspects of works of art. (Visual Art 4.21)
- The student will explain preferences for works of art by responding to aesthetic questions. (Visual Art 4.23)
- The student will: identify and describe representations of points, lines, line segments, rays, and angles, including endpoints and vertices; and identify representations of lines that illustrate intersection, parallelism, and perpendicularity. (Mathematics 4.10)

Vocabulary: Line, Horizontal, Vertical, Diagonal, Parallel, Pattern, Design, Repetition, Negative Space, and Positive Space

Materials: -12" x 12" White paper -Pencil -Eraser -Visual examples -Ruler -*Elements of Design* software -Permanent markers (fine and thick point) -Crayola "Changeable markers" -14" x 14" Colored construction paper (matting)

Procedure:

1) Students are shown examples of artwork (using technology) that contain the types of lines being discussed.
2) Discuss as a class the differences between lines and their direction. Remind students this is part of their current common formative assessment and they will be expected to learn the difference between the lines by the end of the project.
3) Students place a dot on their white paper away from the center of page.

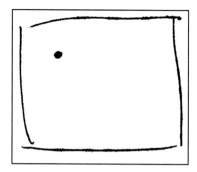

4) From that point they will draw two (only a few inches apart) diagonal lines. (These two lines create a set that will later be filled in with permanent marker. Students may use a pencil to lightly fill in the space to remind them of the area that will later be filled.)

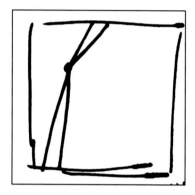

5) They repeat step #4 one more time. All four sets of lines will be coming from a different side of the original point.

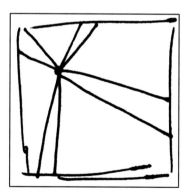

6) Students will draw a set of vertical lines that intersect the lines from steps #4 and #5.

7) Further down the page the student repeats step #5. Note: A set of the vertical lines may end before crossing the entire page.
8) Students will draw a set of horizontal lines that intersect the lines from steps #3 and #4.

9) Further over the page the student repeats step #7. Note: A set of the horizontal lines may end before crossing the entire page.
10) Trace over lines using a fine-tipped "Sharpie."
11) Erase stray pencil marks.
12) Color in lines with thick-tipped permanent marker.

13) Using "Changeable markers," students will choose 3 or 4 colors to fill in the negative space. Avoid placing same colors next to one another.
14) After all negative space is filled in, students will use the "magic wand" to add pattern and design to the already placed colors.
15) Mount artwork on colored paper.
16) Students discuss among tablemates their choices of color and design. They will compare and contrast how each student's work is aesthetically different and that is a celebrated feature of art.

Recommended student reading:

Sir Cumference and the Great Knight of Angleland (A Math Adventure) by Cindy Neuschwander

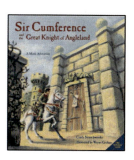

Sonia Delaunay: A Life of Color by Cara Manes

**Recommended student videos:

Elements and Principles of Design by Crystal Productions

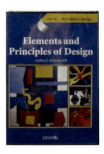

Assessment:

Teacher uses a range of formal and informal assessment strategies to gain insight into students' understanding of lesson, goal achievement, and progress.

Informal:

- Students participate in a class discussion during which questions outlined at the beginning of the lesson are reviewed.
- Individual student-teacher conferences take place during which teacher circulates around classroom assisting students with art project and offering guidance to any questions.
- Teacher observes student work to determine if they used art materials correctly and if they creatively apply skills learned.
- Students participate in a class critique.

Formal:

- Students complete a self-assessment worksheet written in kid-friendly language.
- Teacher completes rubric and uses the tool to evaluate student progress.

**Sample Assessment sheets are located in the book *Appendix*.

Mathematics: Tessellations

Objectives: 5th Grade

- The student will use steps of the art making process, including brainstorming, preliminary sketching, planning, reflecting, and refining, to synthesize ideas for and create works of art. (Visual Art 5.1)
- The student will execute and complete works of art with attention to detail and craftsmanship. (Visual Art 5.2)
- The student will express personal ideas, images, and themes through artistic choices of media, techniques, and subject matter. (Visual Art 5.3)
- The student will identify and apply ethical decisions in art making. (Visual Art 5.4)
- The student will use the following to express meaning in works of art: Balance—formal, informal; Pattern—repetition to create rhythm. (Visual Art 5.5)
- The student will analyze and interpret works of art based on visual properties and context. (Visual Art 5.18)
- The student will analyze an artist's point of view based on contextual information. (Visual Art 5.19)
- The student will use specific criteria to evaluate a finished product. (Visual Art 5.20)
- The student will compare and contrast objects in terms of aesthetic preferences. (Visual Art 5.23)
- The student will reflect on and describe the nature of art. (Visual Art 5.24)
- The student, using plane figures (square, rectangle, triangle, parallelogram, rhombus, and trapezoid), will develop definitions of these plane figures; and investigate and describe the results of combining and subdividing plane figures. (Mathematics 5.13)

Vocabulary: Horizontal, Vertical, Diagonal, Parallel lines, Pattern, Repetition, Polygons, Angles

Materials: -16" x 16" White paper -Pencil -Eraser -Visual examples -Cardstock -Black "Sharpie" -Colored markers -Ruler -18" x 18" Construction paper (matting) -Tessellation pieces

Procedure:

1) Students are shown examples of artwork that contain the types of lines, angles, and shapes being discussed. Review geometry terms: angles and types of lines.
2) Students examine the artwork of M.C. Escher and his tessellation patterns.
3) Students use a piece of cardstock to create a shape or use plastic tessellation pieces (see picture).

4) On a larger piece of paper, students will begin at the top of the corner and trace the shape using a pencil.
5) The shape is then turned over and retraced underneath so that the two shapes touch and are side by side (with no space in between).
6) Students repeat this step until their paper is filled.
7) Trace over the pencil with black "Sharpie" marker.
8) They may add pattern, colors, and design to the shapes.
9) Students mat artwork when complete.
10) Students discuss among tablemates their choices of color and design. Students compare and contrast how each student's work is aesthetically different and that is a celebrated feature of art.

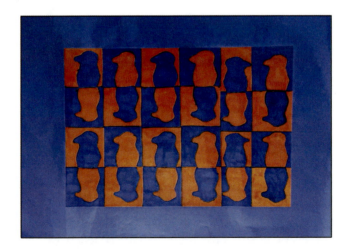

Recommended Student Reading:

The Magic of M. C. Escher by J. L. Locker

Recommended student videos:

Tessellations: How to Create Them by Jim McNeill (Crystal Productions)

M.C. Escher: Master of Graphic Arts (Crystal Productions)

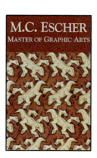

Recommended artwork for lesson demonstration:

- M.C. Escher. *Lizard*. 1942.
- M.C. Escher. *Bird Fish*. 1938.
- M.C. Escher. *Symmetry Drawing*. 1948.
- M.C. Escher. *Horseman*. 1946.
- M.C. Escher. *Fish & Boat*. 1948.

Assessment:

Teacher uses a range of formal and informal assessment strategies to gain insight into students' understanding of lesson, goal achievement, and progress.

Informal:

- Students participate in a class discussion during which questions outlined at the beginning of the lesson are reviewed.
- Individual student-teacher conferences take place during which teacher circulates around classroom assisting students with art project and offering guidance to any questions.
- Teacher observes student work to determine if they used art materials correctly and if they creatively apply skills learned.
- Students participate in a class critique.

Formal:

- Students complete a self-assessment worksheet written in kid-friendly language.
- Teacher completes rubric and uses the tool to evaluate student progress.

**Sample Assessment sheets are located in the book *Appendix*.

5 SUBSTITUTE/RAINY DAY LESSONS

Abstract Flowers Inspired by Georgia O'Keeffe

Objectives: Kindergarten, 1st, 2nd, 3rd, 4th, and 5th Grades

- The student will follow a sequence of steps used in creating works of art. (Visual Art K.3)
- The student will identify and use the following in works of art: Color—primary; Line—wavy; Shape—organic; Pattern—alternating, repeating. (Visual Art 1.7)
- The student will create works of art from observation. (Visual Art 2.9)
- The student will analyze personal works of art, using elements of art and principles of design. (Visual Art 3.19)
- The student will make artistic choices to create compositional unity in works of art. (Visual Art 4.7)
- The student will compare and contrast objects in terms of aesthetic preferences. (Visual Art 5.23)

Vocabulary: Abstract, Warm Colors, Cool Colors, Line, and Repetition

Materials: -8.5" x 11.5" White paper -9" x 12" Colored construction paper -Markers -Black "Sharpie"

Procedure:

1) Draw a circle about 1/3 of the way down on white paper.
2) Draw a scalloped circle around the original circle.

3) Draw 4 wavy lines for the stem. Make sure that they touch the flower top and the bottom of the paper.

4) Draw a small leaf on each side of the stem. Follow the shape of the leaf, draw several larger outlines of the leaf.

5) Repeat the scalloped lines for the flower top until the entire paper has been filled with lines.
6) Repeat the lines for the leaf until the entire bottom of the paper has been filled in with lines.

7) Color the flower in all **<u>warm</u>** colors **OR** all **<u>cool</u>** colors.

Warm Colors **Cool Colors**

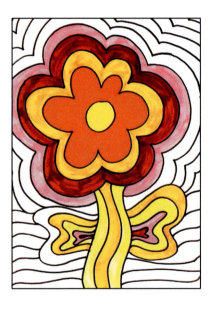 

8) Mat artwork on colored paper.
9) Students discuss among tablemates their choices of color and design. They will compare and contrast how each student's work is aesthetically different and that is a celebrated feature of art.

**Recommended student reading:

Georgia O'Keeffe (Getting to Know the World's Greatest Artists) by Mike Venezia

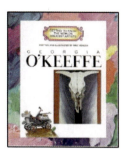

Through Georgia's Eyes by Rachel Rodríguez

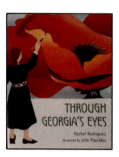

Assessment:

Teacher uses a range of formal and informal assessment strategies to gain insight into students' understanding of lesson, goal achievement, and progress.

Informal:

- Students participate in a class discussion during which questions outlined at the beginning of the lesson are reviewed.
- Individual student-teacher conferences take place during which teacher circulates around classroom assisting students with art project and offering guidance to any questions.
- Teacher observes student work to determine if they used art materials correctly and if they creatively apply skills learned.
- Students participate in a class critique.

Formal:

- Students complete a self-assessment worksheet written in kid-friendly language.
- Teacher completes rubric and uses the tool to evaluate student progress.

**Sample Assessment sheets are located in the book *Appendix*.

Bad Hair Day

Objectives: Kindergarten, 1ˢᵗ, 2ⁿᵈ, 3ʳᵈ, 4ᵗʰ, and 5ᵗʰ Grades

- The student will create works of art that represent personal responses to art-making problems. (Visual Art K.1)
- The student will create art from real and imaginary sources of inspiration. (Visual Art 1.5)
- The student will interpret ideas and feelings expressed in personal and others' works of art. (Visual Art 2.17)
- The student will use imaginative and expressive strategies to create works of art. (Visual Art 3.4)
- The student will make artistic choices to create compositional unity in works of art. (Visual Art 4.7)
- The student will express personal ideas, images, and themes through artistic choices of media, techniques, and subject matter. (Visual Art 5.3)

Vocabulary: Line, Design, Habitat, and Pattern

Materials: -9" x 12" colored construction paper (K-2) -12" x 18" colored construction paper (3-5) -Markers -Pencil -Eraser -Black "Sharpie" -Ruler

Procedure:

1) Create a portrait making hair become subjects of interests. Possible items include: insects, frogs, lizards, dogs, cats, sunshines, underwater scene with fish/shells, plants, flowers, sports, foods, rainforest, art, music, zoo, etc.
2) Begin by drawing the letter "U" with a black "Sharpie". The "U" should be larger than the student's hand.
3) Add two lines for the neck, then add shoulders (Remember shoulders stick our further than the head.)
4) Add a collar or band on shirt.

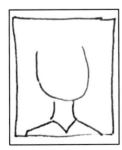 

5) Add ears.
6) Draw ears ½ way down "U". Place nose ½ way down from eyes, mouth ½ way down from nose.

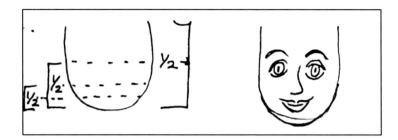

7) Use thick lines, patterns, and repeat design in hair to embellish hair. Make sure to overlap. Possible lines include:

8) Enjoy creating hair design.
9) If students finish early, they may use marker to color in their hair and eyes.
10) Students discuss among tablemates their choices of color and design. They will compare and contrast how each student's work is aesthetically different and that is a celebrated feature of art.

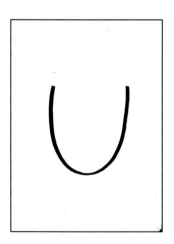 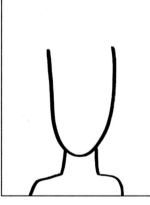 

  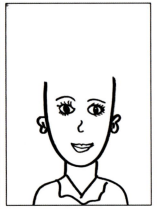

***Recommended Student Reading:**

Crazy Hair Day by Barney Saltzberg

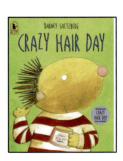

Assessment:

Teacher uses a range of formal and informal assessment strategies to gain insight into students' understanding of lesson, goal achievement, and progress.

Informal:

- Students participate in a class discussion during which questions outlined at the beginning of the lesson are reviewed.
- Individual student-teacher conferences take place during which teacher circulates around classroom assisting students with art project and offering guidance to any questions.
- Teacher observes student work to determine if they used art materials correctly and if they creatively apply skills learned.
- Students participate in a class critique.

Formal:

- Students complete a self-assessment worksheet written in kid-friendly language.
- Teacher completes rubric and uses the tool to evaluate student progress.

**Sample Assessment sheets are located in the book *Appendix*.

Radial Name and Line Design

Objectives: 3rd, 4th, and 5th Grades

- The student will analyze personal works of art, using elements of art and principles of design. (Visual Art 3.19)
- The student will create works of art that connect ideas, art forms, or cultural themes to personal experiences. (Visual Art 4.4)
- The student will make artistic choices to create compositional unity in works of art. (Visual Art 4.7)
- The student will express personal ideas, images, and themes through artistic choices of media, techniques, and subject matter. (Visual Art 5.3)

Vocabulary: Radial Design, Symmetry, Line, Pattern, Design, Repetition, Negative Space, Illusion, Balance, and Rhythm

Materials: -Markers -Changeable markers -White paper (12" x 12") -Pencil. -Eraser -Visual examples -Compass -Circles for tracing

Procedure:

1) Pass out 12" square white paper. Find the center of the paper (does not have to be exact). Draw a dot.

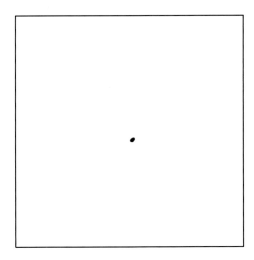

2) With a pencil, LIGHTLY draw three curved lines from the center of the paper to the right edge of the paper. One line near the top, one line that ends in the middle, and one line that ends toward the bottom.

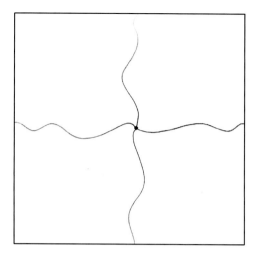

3) Turn paper once clockwise and repeat step #2 LIGHTLY with a pencil. Repeat step #3 until there are three lines going to every side of the paper. (Twelve lines total) Alternate approach: Use a compass and make arcs from center.

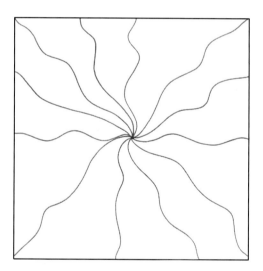

4) Mark every other space LIGHTLY with a mark (x).

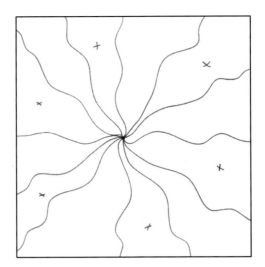

5) In the empty spaces: Start small in the center working out to the wider edge left to right, write first name in one space, last name in next space. Letters must start from the center and go to the edge. Letters must touch both the top and bottom lines. Letters may be block or bubble type letters.
6) There will be four spaces left for lettering after entering first and last name. These spaces should include **positive** adjectives about each student. What are they good at doing (math, science, sports, reading, musical instrument, cheerleader, crossing guard) or something they enjoy (favorite holiday, singing, dancing, eating, baking) or the school they attend.

7) Color in the words using solid colors for the letters and the backgrounds of each space. (One space has all blue letters and a solid orange background, next space has all yellow letters and a black background, etc.).
8) After coloring in all the letters and spaces of the letters, it is time to create the background as a swirl or concentric circles from the center outward. Use a specific pattern of radial colors to create a pattern that begins at the center and expands

completely to the edges of the paper so there is no white showing. If drawing circles, use a large circle for tracing. Trace first with pencil, then go over lines with black "Sharpie." Erase pencil lines.

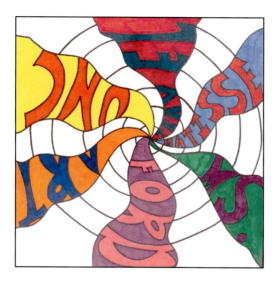

9) Color in circles with marker.
10) Mat artwork.
11) Students discuss among tablemates their choices of color and design. They will compare and contrast how each student's work is aesthetically different and that is a celebrated feature of art.

Recommended student reading:

Children's Book of Art by DK Publishing.

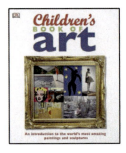

Sonia Delaunay: A Life of Color by Cara Manes

Recommended student video:

(Getting To Know) The Elements of Art

Assessment:

Teacher uses a range of formal and informal assessment strategies to gain insight into students' understanding of lesson, goal achievement, and progress.

Informal:

- Students participate in a class discussion during which questions outlined at the beginning of the lesson are reviewed.

- Individual student-teacher conferences take place during which teacher circulates around classroom assisting students with art project and offering guidance to any questions.
- Teacher observes student work to determine if they used art materials correctly and if they creatively apply skills learned.
- Students participate in a class critique.

Formal:

- Students complete a self-assessment worksheet written in kid-friendly language.
- Teacher completes rubric and uses the tool to evaluate student progress.

**Sample Assessment sheets are located in the book *Appendix*.

APPENDIX A

Science: Clay Frog Lesson Scoring Rubric

	2.1 The student will generate a variety of solutions to art-making problems. (VA Vis.Art)
	2.2 The student will incorporate unanticipated results of art making into works of art. (VA Vis.Art)
	2.5 The student will identify and use the following in works of art: Color—secondary; Form—three-dimensional (cube, cylinder, sphere, pyramid, cone); Shape—geometric, organic. (VA Vis.Art)
	2.10 The student will create three-dimensional works of art, using a variety of materials to include clay. (VA Vis.Art)
	2.4 The student will investigate and understand that plants and animals undergo a series of orderly changes as they mature and grow. Key concepts include: animal life cycles. (VA Science)
	2.5 The student will investigate and understand that living things are part of a system. Key concepts include: living organisms are interdependent with their living and nonliving surroundings; an animal's habitat includes adequate food, water, shelter or cover, and space. (VA Science)

	Needs (1) Improvement	Good (2)	Excellent (3)	Notes	Student Score
2.1 The student will generate a variety of solutions to art-making problems. (O, T, C, Q, P)	Unsuccessfully generated a variety of solutions to art-making problems.	Somewhat generated a variety of solutions to art-making problems.	Successfully generated a variety of solutions to art-making problems.		
2.2 The student will incorporate unanticipated results of art making into works of art. (O, T, P, C,)	Unsuccessfully incorporates unanticipated results of art making into works of art.	Somewhat incorporates unanticipated results of art making into works of art.	Successfully incorporates unanticipated results of art making into works of art.		
2.5 The student will identify and use the following in works of art: Color—secondary; Form—three-dimensional (cube, cylinder, sphere, pyramid, cone); Shape—geometric, organic. (O, C, P, Q)	Unsuccessful in identifying and using the following in works of art: Color—secondary; Form—three-dimensional (cube, cylinder, sphere, pyramid, cone); Shape—geometric, organic.	Somewhat identifies and uses the following in works of art: Color—secondary; Form—three-dimensional (cube, cylinder, sphere, pyramid, cone); Shape—geometric, organic.	Successfully identifies and uses the following in works of art: Color—secondary; Form—three-dimensional (cube, cylinder, sphere, pyramid, cone); Shape—geometric, organic.		

	Needs (1) Improvement	Good (2)	Excellent (3)	Notes	Student Score
2.10 The student will create three-dimensional works of art, using a variety of materials to include clay. (O, C, P)	Unsuccessful in creating a three-dimensional work of art, using a variety of materials to include clay.	Somewhat creates a three-dimensional work of art, using a variety of materials to include clay.	Somewhat creates a three-dimensional work of art, using a variety of materials to include clay.		
2.4 Science. The student will investigate and understand that plants and animals undergo a series of orderly changes as they mature and grow. Key concepts include: animal life cycles. (O, T, Q, P)	Unsuccessful in investigating and understanding that plants and animals undergo a series of orderly changes as they mature and grow.	Somewhat investigates and understands that plants and animals undergo a series of orderly changes as they mature and grow.	Successful in investigating and understanding that plants and animals undergo a series of orderly changes as they mature and grow.		
2.4 Science. The student will investigate and understand that living things are part of a system. Key concepts include: living organisms are interdependent with their living and nonliving surroundings; an animal's habitat includes adequate food, water, shelter or cover, and space. (O, T, C, Q, P)	Unsuccessful in investigating and understanding that living things are part of a system. Key concepts include: living organisms are interdependent with their living and nonliving surroundings; an animal's habitat includes adequate food, water, shelter or cover, and space.	Somewhat investigates and understands that living things are part of a system. Key concepts include: living organisms are interdependent with their living and nonliving surroundings; an animal's habitat includes adequate food, water, shelter or cover, and space.	Successful in investigating and understanding that living things are part of a system. Key concepts include: living organisms are interdependent with their living and nonliving surroundings; an animal's habitat includes adequate food, water, shelter or cover, and space.		
TOTAL					

Assessment Key: (Explains assessment of each standard)
O=Teacher visually observing content and application of technique in artwork (Teacher/Student conference)
T=How students titled their artwork
C=Contributions to art class critique/discussion
Q=Questions on self assessment
P= 3-D clay frog completion

APPENDIX B

Student Self-Critique of Artwork

Art Criticism Assessment	Name_____ Date_____			
Art Criticism	**Rubric and Checklist**	**Good**	**Average**	**Needs Work**
1. DESCRIBE	I have described everything that I have seen in two examples of art in a list. My list includes five details of each work. My spelling is correct. (Back of paper.)			
2. ANALYZE	I have analyzed the work in 2-3 complete sentences to give examples of how each work uses the elements and principles of design. My sentences use correct spelling, punctuation and grammar. (Back of paper.)			
3. INTERPRET	I have interpreted the work, its possible meaning, and why the artist created the piece. (Back of paper.)			
4. DECIDE	Three to five sentences are used to convey the personal judgment or feelings I have about each piece of work. These sentences tell why I decided to like or dislike the works. These opinions are based on personal experience as well as informed judgment. (Back of paper.)			

APPENDIX C

Student Name: _____

<u>**Student Critique of Artwork**</u>

When we <u>study</u>, <u>interpret</u>, and <u>evaluate</u> art, we want to **describe**, **analyze**, **interpret**, and **judge** the artwork. We followed these procedures during our class discussion. Choose a partner and look at their artwork. Think about our discussion and answer the following questions. If you need more space, please write on back of paper. Do your best!

<u>Describe</u>:
Describe what you see in your classmate's artwork.

What type of artwork does your classmate make?

<u>Analyze:</u>
Explain how one of the elements of art is used in the artwork? (line, color, shape, texture, value, space)

Explain how one of the principles of art is used in the artwork? (unity, pattern, balance, rhythm, contrast, emphasis)

<u>Interpret:</u>
Why do you think the artist placed these items in the artwork?

How does the artwork relate to you and your life?

<u>Judge:</u>
Do you like the artwork? Why or why not?

What could make the artwork better?

APPENDIX D

Student Name: _____

<u>Science: Clay Frog Lesson Student Written Self-Assessment</u>

1)   How do you think you did? Circle the face that shows what you think?

       ☹   😐   🙂

2) How would you change your artwork if you had the chance to make it again?

3) What is the title of your artwork?

4) How are art and science related?   Circle the best choice.

    a) We learn about nature and can recreate aspects in art projects.
    b) What we find in nature (frogs) can be found in our artwork.
    c) We can show what we learn about science through drawings, sculptures, and other forms of art.
    d) All of the above.

5) **Draw a pattern in the space below.**

6) We use wooden tools in the clay "frog making" process. Circle the best choice.

      True   False

7) We can shape clay using our fingers and hands. Circle the best choice.

      True   False

8) **Art can be two-dimensional and three-dimensional. Circle the best choice.**

      True   False

9) We can express ourselves through our artwork. Circle the best choice.

      True   False

10) **Why do we make art?**

    a) to express ourselves.
    b) to have something we can look at that shows how we feel and/or what we learned.
    c) to learn more about ourselves and the world around us.
    d) All of the abov

ABOUT THE AUTHOR

Caroline F. Wilson, Ed. D. is an independent art historian whose focus is on modern and contemporary art. She received her B.A. and M.A. degrees in art history from The University of North Carolina-Chapel Hill and The University of South Carolina at Columbia, respectively. While a public school art educator, she earned a doctorate in Educational Leadership from The University of North Carolina-Charlotte. Dr. Wilson resides in Virginia with her husband and young daughter. She enjoys creating pottery in her spare time and maintains an art website at "Artis4everyone.net."

Made in the USA
Monee, IL
04 July 2021